dabble lab

CIRCUIT CREATIONS 4D

MAKE **CIRCUITS**
THAT **GLOW** •OR• **GO**

4D AN AUGMENTED READING EXPERIENCE

by Chris Harbo
and Sarah L. Schuette

CAPSTONE PRESS
a capstone imprint

Dabble Lab is published by Capstone Press,
1710 Roe Crest Drive, North Mankato, Minnesota 56003
www.capstonepub.com

Library of Congress Cataloging-in-Publication Data
Names: Harbo, Christopher L., author. | Schuette, Sarah L., author
Title: Make circuits that glow or go / by Chris Harbo and
   Sarah L. Schuette.
Description: North Mankato, Minnesota : Capstone Press, [2020] | Series:
Dabble lab. Circuit creations 4D | Series: 4D, an augmented
   reading experience | Audience: Age 8–10. | Audience: Grades 4 to 6.
   Identifiers: LCCN 2019008535 | ISBN 9781543539905 (hardcover) |
   ISBN 9781543539943 (paperback) | ISBN 9781543539981 (eBook pdf)
Subjects: LCSH: Light emitting diodes—Juvenile literature. |
   Robots—Juvenile literature. | Electronic circuits—Juvenile literature.
Classification: LCC TK7871.89.L53 H38 2020 | DDC 621.3815—dc23
LC record available at https://lccn.loc.gov/2019008535

Editorial Credits
Abby Colich, editor; Juliette Peters, designer; Jo Miller, media researcher;
Laura Manthe, production assistant

Photo Credits
All photographs by Capstone: Karon Dubke; Marcy Morin and Sarah Schuette,
Project Production; Heidi Thompson, Art Director

Design Elements:
Capstone; Shutterstock: bygermina, rikkyall

All internet sites appearing in back matter were available and accurate when
this book was sent to press.

Printed in the United States of America.
PA70

Download the Capstone app!

- Ask an adult to download the Capstone 4D app.

- Scan the cover and stars inside the book for additional content.

When you scan a spread, you'll find
fun extra stuff to go with this book!
You can also find these things
on the web at www.capstone4D.com
using the password: glow.39905

TABLE OF CONTENTS

●●●●●

SURPRISING CIRCUITS

From flashlights to smartphones, every electrical device you use has a circuit that makes it work. But did you know that circuits aren't just limited to devices you can buy? With common household materials and a few easy steps, you can make a variety of simple, safe, and surprising circuits. Once you master the science of circuits, you can use them in a host of crafts that will amaze others. From glowing luminaries and selfie lights to light-up critters and spinning breakdancers, you'll take circuit creations to a whole new level. So what are you waiting for? The power of circuits is in the palms of your hands!

SAFETY TIPS

While working with circuits and electricity, keep these important safety tips in mind.

- All projects should be done with adult supervision.
- Always disconnect your circuits when not in use.
- Never put batteries in your mouth.
- Never experiment with outlets in the wall.

WHAT IS A CIRCUIT?

In its simplest form, a circuit is a looping path that an electric current flows through. For this path to carry electricity, it often uses four main components. These are a power source, a conductor, a load, and a controller.

Common power sources for circuits are batteries and wall outlets. A conductor is any material, such as metal wire, that can carry electricity. A load is a device, such as a light bulb or motor, that uses the electricity to work. And a controller is a switch that starts or stops the flow of electricity.

For any circuit to work, all four components must be connected in an unbroken loop. When you turn on a flashlight's switch, a closed circuit is created. Electricity flows from the battery, along a wire, through the switch, to the light bulb, and back to the battery. When you flick the flashlight's switch off, a break in the circuit stops the flow of electricity to turn the light bulb off.

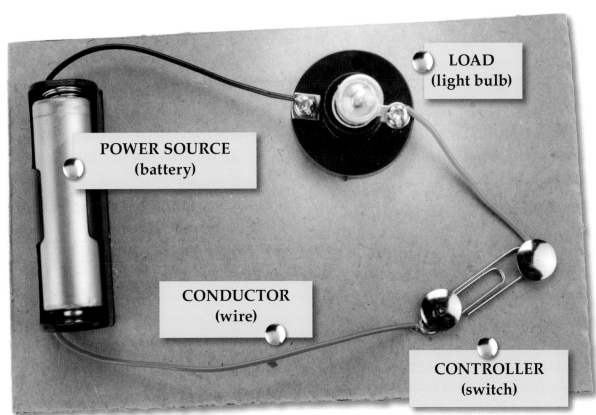

LOAD
(light bulb)

POWER SOURCE
(battery)

CONDUCTOR
(wire)

CONTROLLER
(switch)

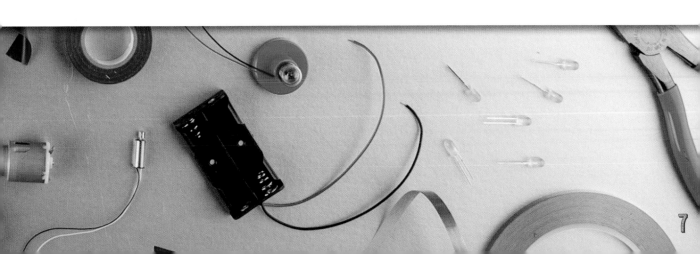

SIMPLE CIRCUITS

Now that you know how circuits work, you can practice connecting them. Then use your imagination to add circuits to common objects and create new things. You can make circuits with a variety of batteries, bulbs, and other easy-to-find items. Use what you have available.

WHAT YOU NEED

AA battery in holder with lead wires
bulb socket and bulb
small screwdriver
insulated wire
wire stripper
2 metal thumbtacks
cardboard
metal paper clip
LED
CR2032 button battery
electrical tape

MAKE IT! ●●●●●

LIGHT UP A LIGHT BULB

1. Connect the black wire from the battery holder to one side of the light bulb socket. If the socket has screws, use them to hold the wire in place.

2. Repeat with the red wire and the other side of the socket. The light bulb will light up!

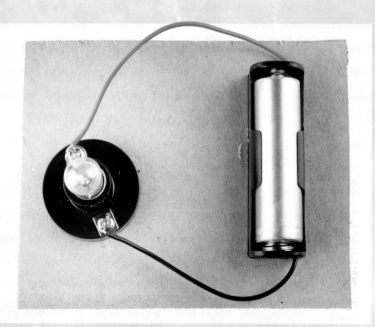

ADD A SWITCH

1. Connect the black wire from the battery holder to one side of the light bulb socket.

2. Cut a piece of wire. Use the wire stripper to strip both ends. Connect one end of the wire to the open side of the socket. Wrap the other end of the wire around a thumbtack. Press the thumbtack into the cardboard.

3. Connect the red wire from the battery holder to the end of a metal paper clip. Press the second thumbtack through the paper clip and into the cardboard. This thumbtack should be a short distance from the first thumbtack.

4. Move the paper clip to open and close the circuit and turn the light bulb on and off.

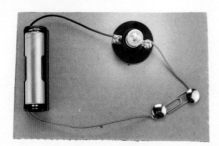

LIGHT UP AN LED

1. Slide an LED bulb onto a button battery. The long leg should touch the positive (+) side of the battery. The short leg should touch the negative (-) side.

2. Wrap electrical tape around the battery to hold the LED in place.

TIP!

Cut a small piece from a plastic lid. Slide it under an LED leg to turn the light off. Remove it to turn it back on.

STRIPPING WIRES

Before you begin making circuits, practice stripping wires. To strip, or remove the coating on the end of a wire, use a wire stripper. Line up the wire size with the same size hole on the stripper. Press down lightly to cut into the coating without cutting the wire. Then pull the stripper away from your body.

LANDSCAPE LUMINARIES

Now you can add drama to your dioramas. With a couple of simple circuits, buildings and trees will light up your landscapes.

WHAT YOU NEED

small screwdriver
AA battery in holder with lead wires
light bulb socket
cardboard box
scissors
paint, markers, and craft materials
clear tape
wax paper
CR2032 button battery
LED
cone-shaped paper cup
electrical tape

MAKE IT!

1. Use a screwdriver to connect the battery holder's red wire to one side of the light bulb socket and the black wire to the other side. The light bulb will light up.

2. Cut holes in a small cardboard box to look like windows and doors. Use paint, markers, or other craft materials to decorate the box to look like a house.

3. Tape wax paper over the holes on the inside of the box.

4. Set your house over the circuit.

5. Slide a button battery between the legs of an LED. The long leg should be on the positive (+) side of the battery and the short leg on the negative (-) side.

6. Secure the LED's legs to the button battery with electrical tape.

7. Place a cone-shaped paper cup over the button battery circuit to make a tree.

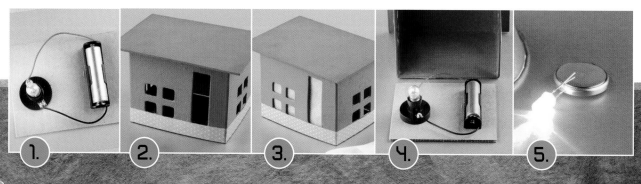

1.   2.   3.   4.   5.

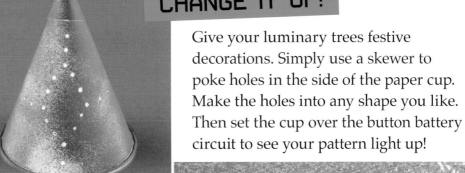

CHANGE IT UP!

Give your luminary trees festive decorations. Simply use a skewer to poke holes in the side of the paper cup. Make the holes into any shape you like. Then set the cup over the button battery circuit to see your pattern light up!

CIRCUIT SAFARI

Take your circuitry skills on a safari. By adding a few glowing eyes, you'll put the "wild" in your wildlife.

WHAT YOU NEED

scissors
paper towel tube
paint and craft supplies
craft knife
CR2032 button battery
2 LEDs
electrical tape

MAKE IT!

1. Use a scissors to cut a paper tube into an animal shape, such as a cobra. Decorate your animal with paint and craft supplies

2. Poke two eye holes in your animal shape with a craft knife.

3. Slide an LED bulb through each of the holes. The bulbs should be on the outside of the head.

4. In the back of the animal, slide a button battery between the legs of the LEDs. The long legs should be on the positive (+) side of the battery and the short legs on the negative (-) side.

5. Secure the legs of the LEDs to the button battery with electrical tape. The animal's eyes will light up.

6. Repeat steps 1 through 5 to make more animals to fill out your safari scene.

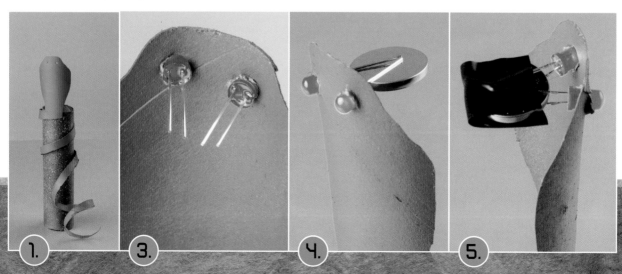

1.   3.   4.   5.

CHANGE IT UP!

Add LED eyes to your favorite origami animal. Make paper bats with glowing red eyes for Halloween.

SELFIE LAMP

Don't get left out in the dark. Build a selfie lamp to help you take the perfect pics—in low light or no light!

WHAT YOU NEED

LED
CR2032 button battery
electrical tape
domed plastic cup lid
scissors
cardstock
hot glue gun
clothespin

MAKE IT!

1. Slide a button battery between the legs of an LED. The long leg should be on the positive (+) side of the battery and the short leg on the negative (-) side.

2. Secure the LED's legs to the button battery with several layers of electrical tape.

3. Use a scissors to cut a square of cardstock that is slightly larger than the hole in the domed lid. Tape the cardstock over the hole in the lid.

4. Use a craft knife to cut a small X in the center of the cardstock.

5. Slide the bulb end of button battery circuit through the X in the cardstock. Secure the circuit with electrical tape.

6. Hot glue the clothespin to the back of the lid.

7. Clip the selfie lamp to your smartphone and start taking pictures!

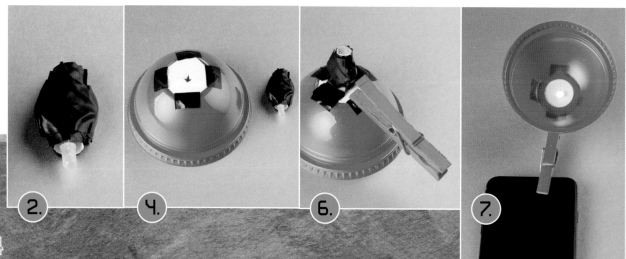

2.   4.   6.   7.

CHANGE IT UP!

Clip this light to any tablet, or use it as a reading light for your favorite book. Make a few of these lights and give them as gifts.

PENCIL LIGHT

Shed a little light on your favorite subject. With a pencil light, you can keep on writing long after the lights go out.

WHAT YOU NEED

LED
CR2032 button battery
scissors
plastic lid
electrical tape
small plastic cup
pencil
hot glue gun
small clothespin

MAKE IT!

1. Slide a button battery between the legs of an LED. The long leg should be on the positive (+) side of the battery and the short leg on the negative (-) side.

2. Cut a small strip out of the plastic lid. Slide the plastic strip under one leg of the LED.

3. Secure the LED's legs to the button battery with several layers of electrical tape. Slide the plastic strip in and out to turn the LED on and off.

4. Cut the bottom off a small plastic cup.

5. Use a pencil to poke a hole in the cup bottom. Push the LED bulb through the hole. Secure the circuit to the cup with electrical tape.

6. Glue the clothespin to the taped circuit.

7. Clip the clothespin to the pencil. Now you can write in the dark!

3.   5.   6.

SIMPLE CONDUCTOR CIRCUITS

Graphite, copper, foil, and other elements are good conductors for electricity. Electricity can flow through them, and they can be used to make paths for electricity. These paths are called traces. The best way to practice these circuits is on paper. Once you learn the basics, you can experiment with them on other surfaces.

WHAT YOU NEED

graphite pencil (2B or harder)
paper
LEDs
clear tape
9-volt battery
CR2032 button battery
copper tape

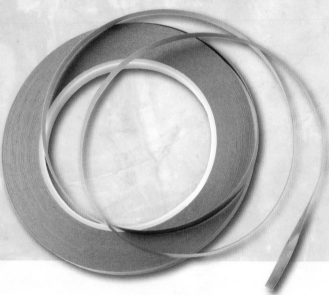

MAKE IT! ●●●●●

GRAPHITE CIRCUIT

1. With the graphite pencil, draw two parallel lines. Mark the ends of one line with positive (+) symbols. Then mark the other line with negative (-) symbols.

2. Open the legs of the LED. Tape each leg to one end of your lines. The long leg should touch the line with the positive (+) symbol. The short leg should touch the line with the negative (-) symbol.

3. Set the connection ports of the 9-volt battery on the other end of your lines. Match up the positive and negative ports of the battery to the markings on your drawing.

4. The LED will light up if the circuit is connected correctly. You may need to check the circuit in a dark place. The LED will be dimmer than lights from other circuits.

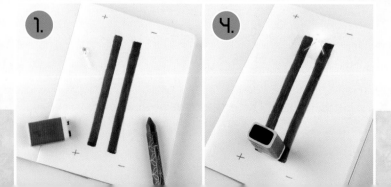

COPPER TAPE CIRCUIT

1. Use the graphite pencil to sketch a circuit path with two openings.

2. Remove the backing of the copper tape. Stick the copper tape on top of your sketch.

3. Spread the legs of the LED and tape them to the copper tape at one of the circuit's openings. One leg should connect to each end of copper tape.

4. At the second opening, place a button battery on top of one end of the copper tape. Then fold the corner of the paper over so the other end of the copper tape touches the top of the battery. Watch the LED light up.

CIRCUIT PENS AND PAINT

Experimenting with circuit writer pens and paint can be a lot of fun. Circuit pens can be found in craft stores. They work by drawing over the top of your graphite sketches. Once your traced lines are dry, just connect a battery and LED and watch the LED light up.

Circuit paint can be made by mixing the same amounts of liquid graphite powder and acrylic paint. Once again, just trace over your graphite circuits with the conductive paint, let it dry, and then hook up your components.

TIP!

Before you use copper tape, cut a small piece and remove the backing. Does the tape look the same on both sides? If it does, then both sides of the tape are conductive. Some copper tape is only conductive on one side. Be very careful with copper tape. The edges can be sharp.

BRIGHT IDEA JOURNAL

Collect your best and brightest ideas all in one place—then show everyone how they shine!

WHAT YOU NEED

journal
markers and crayons
circuitry scraps
graphite pencil (2B or harder)
LED
clear tape
9-volt battery
copper tape (optional)
conductive paint (optional)
circuit pen (optional)

MAKE IT!

1. Decorate the cover of your circuitry journal. Consider using markers or crayons to draw pictures of circuit materials, such as light bulbs, wires, or batteries. Or try gluing circuit scraps to the cover to give your journal a high-tech vibe!

2. Open your circuit journal and draw your first simple conductive circuit. Start with a long winding line. Label each end of the line with a positive (+) symbol.

3. Draw a second winding line alongside the first one. Keep the lines about a thumb's width apart. When you're done, your drawing should look like a winding path. Label the ends of the second line with negative (-) symbols.

4. Open the legs of the LED. Tape each leg to one opening of your winding path. The long leg should touch the positive (+) symbol, and the short leg should touch the negative (-) symbol.

5. Set the connection ports of the 9-volt battery on the second opening of your path. Match up the positive and negative ports of the battery to the markings on your drawing. Your LED should light up.

6. Continue drawing circuit ideas in your new journal. Experiment with copper tape, conductive paint, and circuit pens to see how many amazing designs you can make shine!

2.

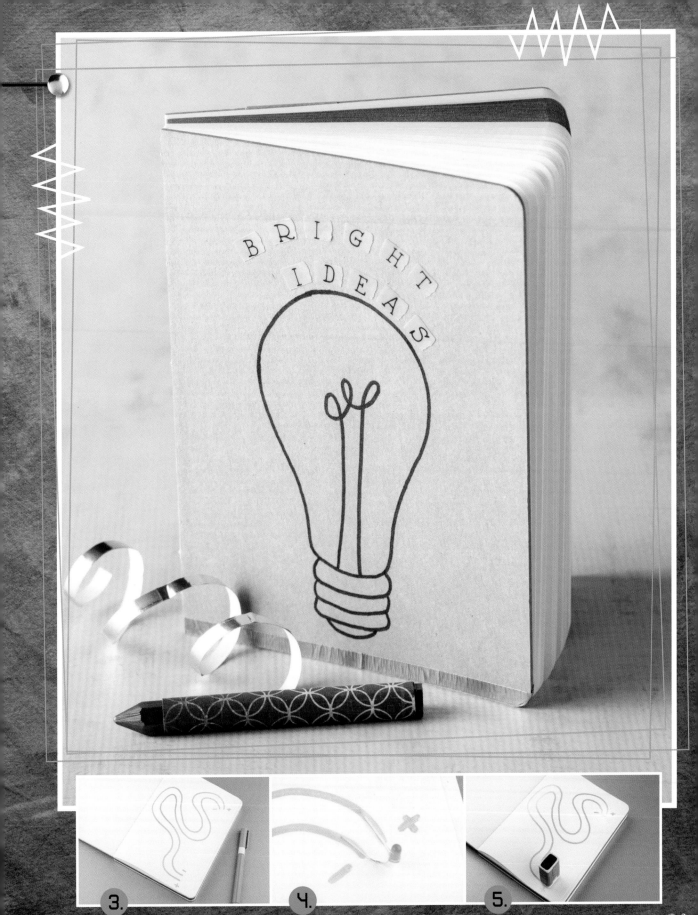

SALT AND DOUGH CIRCUITS

Just like graphite and copper, salt is a great conductor. When made into dough, you can make circuits with it. You can buy conductive dough in craft stores or you can make your own.

CONDUCTIVE DOUGH

WHAT YOU NEED

1 ½ cups (210 grams) flour, plus extra
   for dusting
1 cup (240 milliliters) water
¼ cup (48 g) salt
½ cup (120 mL) lemon juice
1 tablespoon (15 mL) vegetable oil
food coloring
saucepan
wooden spoon
cutting board

1.

3.

MAKE IT! ●●●●●

1. Set aside ½ cup (70 g) of flour. Mix the other 1 cup (140 g) of flour, water, salt, lemon juice, vegetable oil, and food coloring together in the saucepan.

2. Place the pan on the stove. Heat it on medium, stirring constantly.

3. Keep stirring. The mixture will start to get thicker. Stir until it forms a ball.

4. Dust a cutting board with flour. Remove the dough from the saucepan and place it on the cutting board.

5. Dust more flour on top of the dough ball. Flatten the ball with your spoon. Let cool at least five minutes.

6. Start kneading the ½ cup (70 g) of flour into the dough ball. Keep kneading until the dough is smooth and not sticky.

7. After the conductive dough cools, store it in a plastic bag for up to one week.

5.

6.

23

INSULATING DOUGH

WHAT YOU NEED

1 ½ cups (210 g) flour, plus extra for dusting
½ cup (95 g) sugar
3 tablespoons (45 mL) vegetable oil
½ cup (120 mL) water
food coloring
mixing bowl
wooden spoon
cutting board

MAKE IT!

1. Set aside ½ cup (70 g) of flour. Pour the other 1 cup (140 g) of flour, sugar, and vegetable oil in a bowl and mix together.

2. Add food coloring to the water. Pour little amounts of water into the bowl and mix. Repeat until the dough forms a ball.

3. Dust a cutting board with flour. Place the dough ball on the cutting board.

4. Sprinkle more flour on top of the dough. Knead the dough until it is smooth and no longer sticky.

5. Store your insulating dough in a plastic bag for up to one week.

1.

2.

WHAT YOU NEED

conductive dough
LED
9-volt battery in holder with lead wires

MAKE IT! ●●●●●

1. Form two shapes, such as stars, out of conductive dough. Set them side by side without touching.

2. Stick the red wire from the battery holder into one dough shape. Stick the black wire into the other dough shape.

3. Open the legs of an LED. Stick the long leg into the dough with the red wire. Stick the short leg into the dough with the black wire. The LED will light up!

3.

TIP!

If you don't want gaps between your conductive dough—or you need to layer it—place insulating dough between the conductive dough to allow the circuit to work.

25

HAPPY BIRTHDAY CANDLE

Dress up your next birthday party with electric table decorations. Make the conductive and insulating doughs first, and then see your cupcake and candle shine!

WHAT YOU NEED

conductive dough
insulating dough
LED
9-volt battery in holder with leads

MAKE IT!

1. Make a cupcake-shaped base out of conductive dough.

2. Roll another piece of conductive dough into a long rope. Wind the dough rope on top of the cupcake base to look like frosting.

3. Form a piece of insulating dough into a small disk shape. Set it on top of the conductive frosting.

4. Blend two colors of conductive dough and form into a candle shape. Stick the candle to the small disk of insulating dough.

5. Slide the short leg of the LED into the candle and the long leg into the frosting. Bend the LED legs as necessary to fit.

6. Connect the battery holder's black wire to the candle and the red wire to the frosting. Your candle will light up!

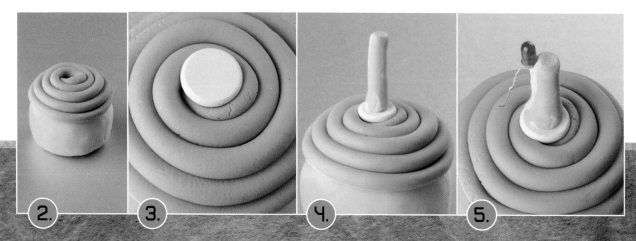

2.   3.   4.   5.

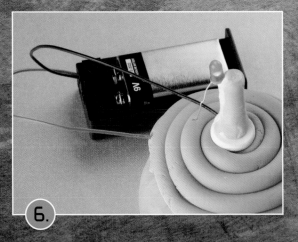

6.

CHANGE IT UP!

Be creative with your conductive dough circuits. Challenge yourself to make animals with glowing eyes, vehicles with headlights, or even flying saucers trimmed with lights. The possibilities are endless!

SIMPLE SALTWATER CIRCUIT

Dough isn't the only material salt can be used in to conduct electricity. Try your hand at building a simple saltwater circuit.

WHAT YOU NEED

2 craft sticks
aluminum foil
1 red wire with alligator clips
1 black wire with alligator clips
plastic cup
salt
9-volt battery in holder with lead wires and alligator clips
light bulb socket and bulb
eyedropper
water

MAKE IT

1. Wrap the two craft sticks in foil. These are electrodes. Clip the red wire to one electrode and the black wire to the other electrode.

2. Fill the bottom of a plastic cup with salt, about two finger-widths deep. Slide the electrodes into the salt. Make sure they do not touch.

3. Clip the red wire on one of the electrodes to the battery pack's black wire. Clip the battery pack's red wire to one side of the bulb socket.

4. Clip the black wire from the other electrode to the other side of the bulb socket.

5. Use an eyedropper to add drops of water to the salt. Watch the light bulb light up!

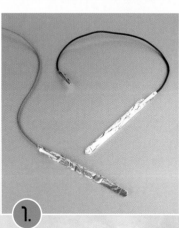

1.

2.

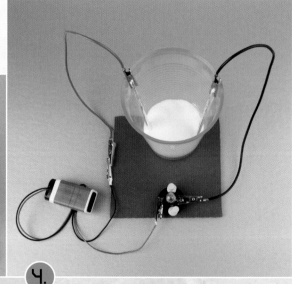

4.

CHANGE IT UP!

Try putting water in the cup first. Then add salt to the water. How much salt does it take for the bulb to light up? Or try filling the cup with lemon juice instead of saltwater. What happens?

SPACE COLONY

Shoot for the moon with this circuit-powered scene!
Your light-up space colony will look out of this world!

WHAT YOU NEED

small plastic cup
craft knife
3 small craft sticks
aluminum foil
hot glue gun
2 wires with alligator clips
light bulb socket and bulb
9-volt battery in holder with wire leads
electrical tape
domed plastic cup lid
large bowl
small bowl
1 cup (190 g) salt
1 tablespoon (15 mL) water

MAKE IT!

1. Cut a hole in the bottom of the plastic cup
   with a craft knife. Wrap each craft stick
   in foil. Hot glue them to the cup.

2. Slide the light bulb through the hole in
   the domed lid and secure the socket with
   electrical tape.

3. Feed the socket's lead wires through the
   hole in the cup. Hot glue the lid to the
   cup to make it look like a satellite dish.

4. Connect the light bulb socket's red wire
   to one foil leg with electrical tape.

5. Clip one wire with an alligator clip to
   the leg with the red wire. Clip the wire's
   other end to the battery.

6. Clip the other wire with an alligator clip
   to the black wire from the socket. Clip
   the wire's other end to the battery.

7. Set the small bowl inside the large bowl.
   Pour salt into the small bowl. Set your
   satellite dish on top of the salt. Add a
   small amount of water to the salt. The
   satellite dish will light up!

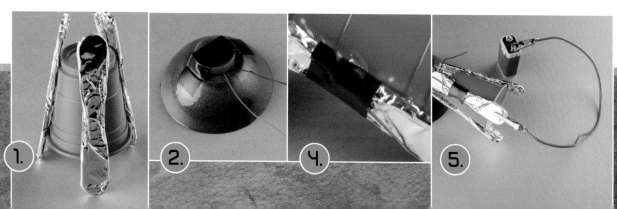

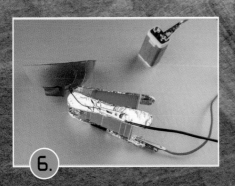

6.

DECORATE IT!

Make a space zen garden to go with your satellite. Add moon rocks and colorful sand. Don't forget to add an astronaut or space creature!

MOVING CIRCUITS

Now that you can connect simple circuits, let's make circuits that move! Batteries store energy for use when you need it. Magnets can be used to make electricity. They can work independently or together in the circuits you create.

WHAT YOU NEED

low-speed hobby motor
AA batteries in holder with switches
     and lead wires
mini vibrating motor
CR2032 button battery
neodymium magnets
AA battery
copper wire
needle-nose pliers

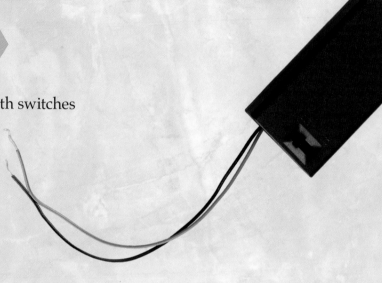

MAKE IT!

POWER A MOTOR

1. Connect the black wire from the battery holder to the red wire from the motor. Then connect the remaining two wires the same way.

2. Wrap and secure both connections with electrical tape.

3. Switch on the battery pack and watch the shaft on the motor spin!

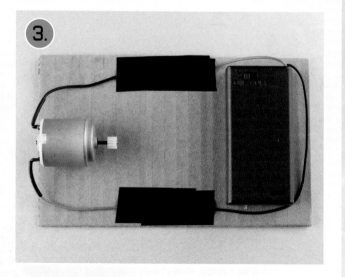

CONNECT A MINI VIBRATING MOTOR

1. Connect the black wire from the mini vibrating motor to the negative (-) side of the button battery. Secure the connection with electrical tape.

2. Connect the red wire from the motor to the positive (+) side of the battery. Watch the motor wiggle!

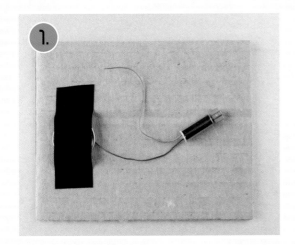

MAKE A HOMOPOLAR MOTOR

1. Stack the neodymium magnets on top of each other.

2. Set the AA battery on top of the magnets, positive (+) side down.

3. Wrap the copper wire down around the battery to make a coil. The coil should be loose around the battery and magnet stack.

4. Use a needle-nose pliers to bend a small dip at the top of your wire coil.

5. Balance the dip on top of the battery and watch the wire coil spin!

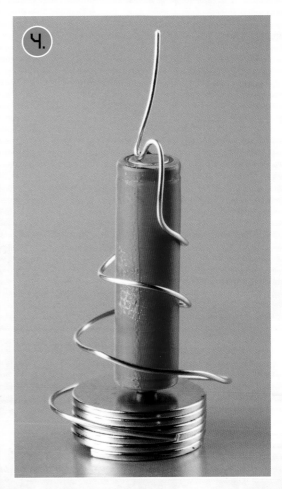

FOOD BOTS

You can make food bots out of anything! Look around your house and in your recycling bin for ideas!

WHAT YOU NEED

mini vibrating motor
CR2032 button battery
hot glue gun
clean fast food containers
peanut butter jar lid
electrical tape

MAKE IT!

1. Place the vibrating motor's red wire on the positive (+) side of the button battery. Secure the connection to the underside of the jar lid with electrical tape.

2. Slide the motor's black wire onto the negative (-) side of the battery. The motor will wiggle! Then disconnect the black wire while you build the rest of the project.

3. Glue a fast food container to the top of the lid. Fill it with real or pretend food.

4. Reconnect the black wire under the lid. Flip the lids over on a table and watch your food bot wiggle with excitement!

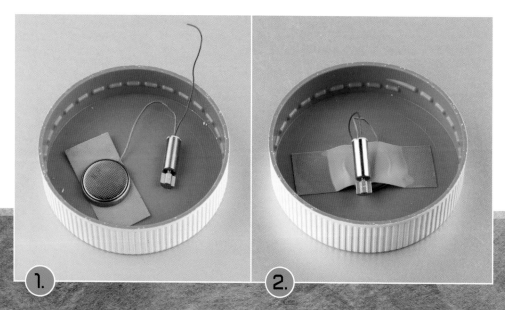

CARNIVAL CREATIONS

Everyone loves a carnival! Create your own with flying swings and a spinning scrambler that move!

WHAT YOU NEED

scissors
cardboard
awl
2 low-speed hobby motors with leads
2 AA battery holders with leads
　　and switches
electrical tape
paper cup
craft knife
7 paper treat boats
string
oatmeal container with lid
craft knife
paper punch
hot glue gun

MAKE IT!

1. Use a scissors to cut two cardboard circles, about the size of a plate. Leave a strip of cardboard in the center of each circle.

2. Use an awl to poke a small hole in the center of each circle's cardboard strip. These holes will slide onto the motors' shafts later in the project.

3. Connect the black wire from one battery holder to the red wire of one motor. Then connect the remaining two wires. Wrap the connections with electrical tape.

4. Repeat step 3 with the other battery holder and motor.

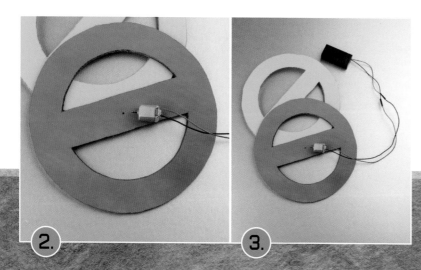

2.

3.

5. Use a craft knife to cut a hole in the bottom of the paper cup that is just large enough to fit a motor.

6. Place one of the motors into the hole in the paper cup. Then slide the motor's shaft into the small hole (made in step 2) of one of the cardboard circles.

7. Repeat steps 5 and 6 with the plastic lid from the oatmeal container and the remaining motor.

8. To make the swing ride, cut the paper treat boats in half. Then punch holes into the sides of each half with a paper punch.

9. Thread strings through the holes and tie them around the cardboard circle connected to the motor in the oatmeal lid. Place the lid on the oatmeal container. The paper boats will hang down like swings.

10. To make the scrambler, glue four paper treat boats to the circle connected to the motor in the paper cup.

11. Switch on the battery packs and watch the rides spin!

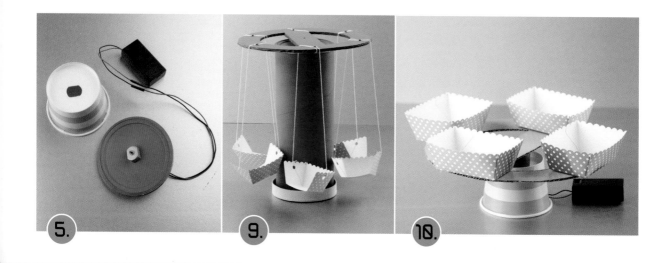

5.　　　9.　　　10.

CHANGE IT UP!

Decorate your whirling rides with painted paper cups, flags, and other craft materials. You could even add button battery circuits with LEDs to light them up!

ROBOT GEAR PACK

All good gadget builders need a special bag for their gear. Now you can design a circuit-driven gear pack that reflects your maker style.

WHAT YOU NEED

scissors
cardboard
hot glue gun
gears and other robot-themed parts
plastic propeller
low-speed hobby motor
electrical tape
square piece of scrap wood
AA batteries in battery pack with
    switch and lead wires
backpack

MAKE IT!

1. Use a scissors to cut a face shape and a small circle out of cardboard. Glue gears and other robot-themed parts to the front of the circle.

2. Glue a propeller to the back of the circle.

3. Push the motor's shaft through the back of the cardboard face and secure the motor with electrical tape. Then slide the circle's propeller onto the motor's shaft.

4. Glue the scrap wood to the bottom of the cardboard face.

5. Attach the red wire from the motor to the black wire on the battery pack. Then connect the remaining two wires and wrap both connections with electrical tape.

6. Slide the wood piece into the front pocket of a backpack. Then turn on the battery pack's switch to see the circle spin!

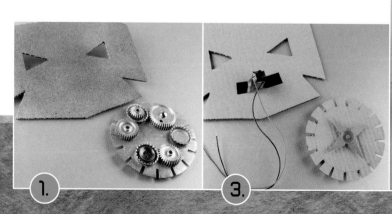

1.

3.

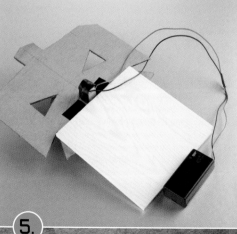

5.

CHANGE IT UP!

Decorate your gear pack with a variety
of fun materials. Old puzzle pieces and
corrugated cardboard make cool add-ons.
You could even add a simple circuit with
a light bulb socket to brighten things up.

ELECTROMAGNETIC TRAIN

All aboard! Use your circuit-making magic to create an electromagnetic train of your very own.

WHAT YOU NEED

copper wire
wood dowel
AA battery
6 small neodymium magnets

MAKE IT!

1. Coil the copper wire tightly around a wooden dowel. Remove the dowel. The wire coil should look like a big spring.

2. Stick three magnets on each end of the battery. The magnets should be slightly wider than the battery.

3. Set the battery inside the wire coil and watch it zoom!

TIP!

Hold the two stacks of magnets to make sure they repel each other before putting them on the battery.

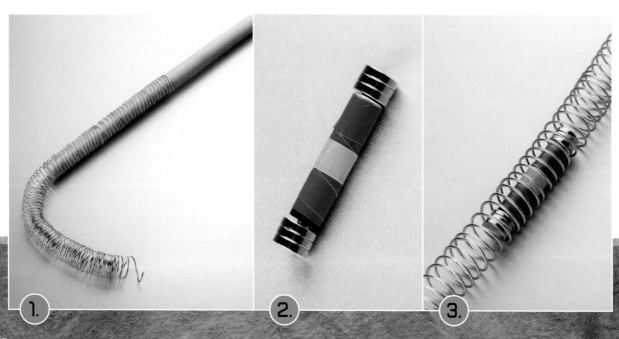

1.   2.   3.

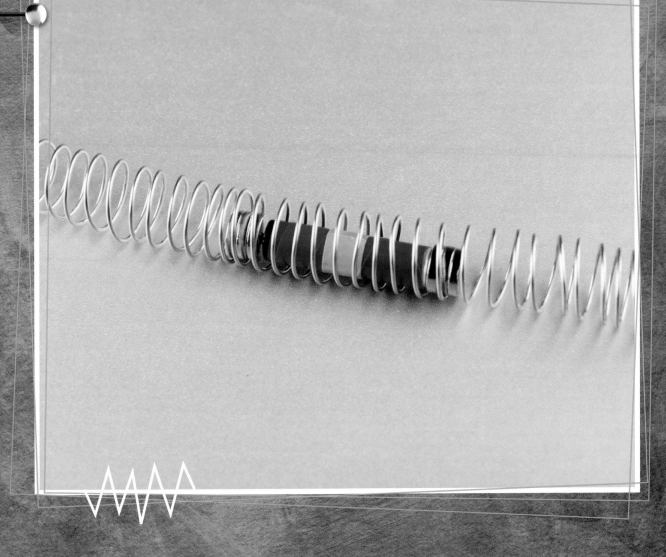

BE CAREFUL!

Neodymium magnets can be found online. They're very strong, so be careful using them. They will break or shatter if you let them snap together. If you have a pacemaker or other health device, use caution or avoid doing projects with neodymium magnets.

BREAKDANCER

Amaze your friends by giving this breakdancer a spin. It's sure to be the life of the party!

WHAT YOU NEED

neodymium magnets
AA battery
marker
paper
needle-nose pliers
copper wire

MAKE IT!

1. Stack the neodymium magnets on top of each other. Set the AA battery on top of the magnets, positive (+) side down.

2. Sketch an outline of a breakdancer on a piece of paper. Then use the needle-nose pliers to bend the copper wire into that shape.

3. Use the pliers to bend a small dip at the bottom of your shape.

4. Wrap the wire down around the battery to make a coil. The coil should be loose around the battery and magnet stack.

5. Balance the dip on top of the battery. Watch your superhero spin!

TIP!

Make sure your wire coils do not touch and that your shape is balanced. If it doesn't spin right away, just keep adjusting the wire until it does.

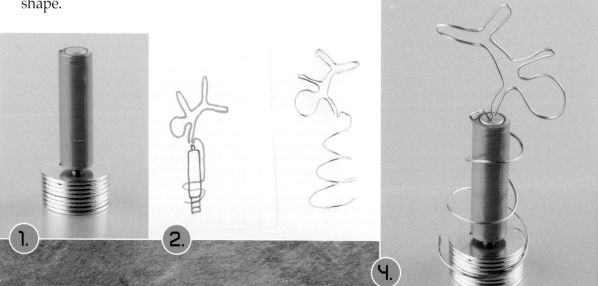

1.
2.
4.

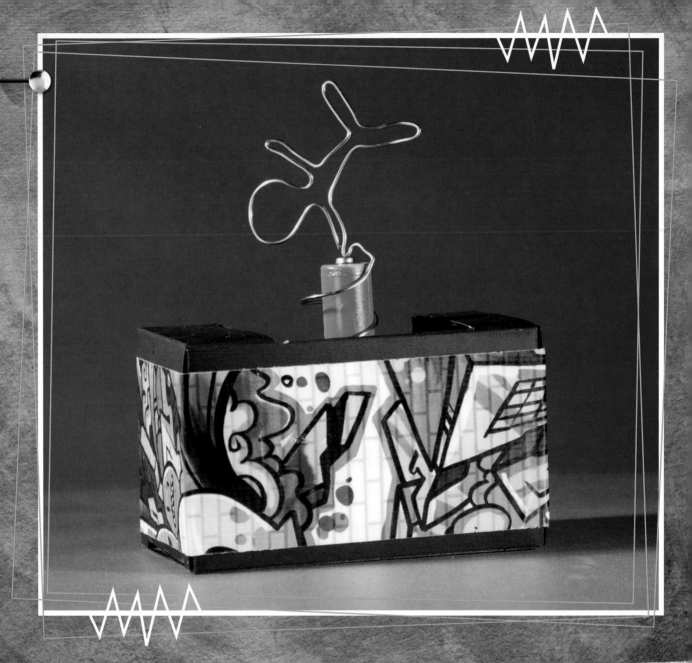

DECORATE IT!

Decorate a small box with paint or duct tape to look like a stage or city street.

CHANGE IT UP!

Flip your battery over and put the negative side (-) on top of the magnet. What happens? In which direction does the breakdancer spin?

GLOSSARY

battery (BA-tuh-ree)—a container holding chemicals that store and create electricity

button battery (BUHT-uhn BA-tuh-ree)—a small, disc-shaped battery

colony (KAH-luh-nee)—an area that has been settled by people from another country

component (kuhm-POH-nuhnt)—a part of a machine or system

conductor (kuhn-DUHK-tuhr)—a material that lets heat, electricity, or sound travel easily through it

controller (kuhn-TROHL-uhr)—a switch or other mechanism in a circuit that starts and stops the flow of electricity

current (KUHR-uhnt)—a flow of electrons through an object

diorama (dy-uh-RA-muh)—a three-dimensional replication of a scene, often in miniature

electromagnetic (i-lek-troh-mag-NET-ik)—having to do with a temporary magnet formed when electricity flows through a coil of wire

gadget (GAJ-it)—a small tool that does a particular job

graphite (GRAF-ite)—a black or gray mineral in pencils; graphite is the part of a pencil used for writing

insulator (IN-suh-lay-tur)—material that does not allow electricity to flow through

LED (EL-EE-DEE)—a type of light; LED stands for light-emitting diode

load (LOHD)—a device to which power is delivered

luminary (LOO-min-air-ee)—a decorative light

magnet (MAG-nit)—a piece of metal that attracts iron or steel

neodymium magnet (nee-oh-DIME-ee-um MAG-nit)—a very strong, permanent magnet made up of the elements neodymium, iron, and boron

switch (SWICH)—the part of a circuit that turns electrical objects on or off; a switch creates a gap in a circuit

Nydal Dahl, Oyvind. *A Beginner's Guide to Circuits: Nine Simple Projects with Lights, Sounds, and More!* San Francisco: No Starch Press, 2018.

Olson, Elsie. *Connect It! Circuits You Can Squish, Bend, and Twist.* Cool Makerspace Gadgets and Gizmos. Minneapolis: Abdo, 2018.

Roland, James. *How Circuits Work.* Connect with Electricity. Minneapolis: Lerner, 2017.

INTERNET SITES

DK Find Out: Circuits
https://www.dkfindout.com/us/science/electricity/circuits

Left Brain, Craft Brain: Circuit Activities for Kids
https://leftbraincraftbrain.com/circuit-activities-kids

Science Games for Kids: Electricity Circuits
http://www.sciencekids.co.nz/gamesactivities/electricitycircuits.html

TITLES IN THIS SET:

A **4D** BOOK

MAKE **ART** WITH **CIRCUITS**

BY CHRIS HARBO AND SARAH L. SCHUETTE

A **4D** BOOK

MAKE **CIRCUITS** YOU CAN **WEAR**

BY CHRIS HARBO AND SARAH L. SCHUETTE

A **4D** BOOK

MAKE **CIRCUITS** THAT **GLOW** OR **GO**

BY CHRIS HARBO AND SARAH L. SCHUETTE

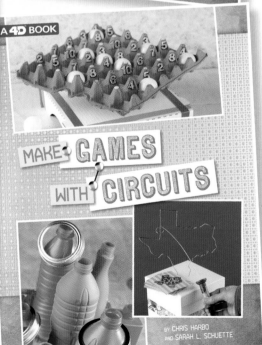

A **4D** BOOK

MAKE **GAMES** WITH **CIRCUITS**

BY CHRIS HARBO AND SARAH L. SCHUETTE